DATE DUE

JUN 0 5 2013

# POLLUTION

By Barbara Linde

Gareth Stevens
Publishing

Please visit our website, www.garethstevens.com. For a free color catalog of all our high-quality books, call toll free 1-800-542-2595 or fax 1-877-542-2596.

**Library of Congress Cataloging-in-Publication Data**

Linde, Barbara M.
Pollution / by Barbara M. Linde.
 p. cm. — (Habitat havoc)
Includes index.
ISBN 978-1-4339-9857-7 (pbk.)
ISBN 978-1-4339-9928-4 (6-pack)
ISBN 978-1-4339-9926-0 (library binding)
1. Pollution — Juvenile literature. 2. Refuse and refuse disposal — Juvenile literature. I. Linde, Barbara M. II. Title.
TD176.L56 2014
363.73—dc23

First Edition

Published in 2014 by
**Gareth Stevens Publishing**
111 East 14th Street, Suite 349
New York, NY 10003

Copyright © 2014 Gareth Stevens Publishing

Designer: Andrea Davison-Bartolotta
Editor: Kristen Rajczak

Photo credits: Cover, p. 1 R. Gino Santa Maria/Shutterstock.com; pp. 4, 17 (inset), 26 iStockphoto/Thinkstock; p. 5 think4photop/Shutterstock.com; p. 6 TonyV3112/Shutterstock.com; p. 7 David Hiser/Stone/Getty Images; pp. 8–9 Christopher Wood/Shutterstock.com; p. 11 (main) Boisvieux Christophe/hemis.fr/Getty Images; p. 11 (inset) Feng Li/Getty Images; pp. 12–13 De Agostini Picture Library/De Agostini/Getty Images; pp. 14–15 Christophe Simon/AFP/Getty Images; p. 15 (inset) Martin Harvey/Peter Arnold/Getty Images; p. 17 (main) Operation Shooting/Shutterstock.com; p. 19 Mary Plage/Oxford Scientific/Getty Images; p. 21 (both) Universal Images Group via Getty Images; p. 22 Petty Officer 1st Class David C. Lloyd, US Navy/Defense.gov/Wikimedia Commons; p. 23 (inset) Dorling Kindersley/Getty Images; p. 23 (main) Konrad Wothe/Picture Press/Getty Images; pp. 24–25 Maciej Frolow/Photodisc/Getty Images; p. 27 (main) Paul Prescott/Shutterstock.com; p. 27 (inset) Digital Vision/Thinkstock; p. 28 Douglas Graham/Roll Call/Getty Images; p. 29 Pavel L Photo and Video/Shutterstock.com.

Printed in the United States of America

CPSIA compliance information: Batch #CW14GS: For further information contact Gareth Stevens, New York, New York at 1-800-542-2595.

# Contents

Words in the glossary appear in **bold** type the first time they are used in the text.

# YUCK! DO YOU SEE THAT?

It's a hot summer day, and you've finally arrived at the beach for your summer vacation. You look forward to spending lots of time in the cool water. Maybe you'll build a sand castle.

Your first sight of the beach is a shock. There's a big pile of trash on one of the sandbanks. Closer to the water, you see the remains of a bonfire, complete with burnt wood, cans, and food wrappers. A few seagulls are picking through the **debris**. A couple of plastic trash bags are bobbing in the water.

You wonder: How can people leave such a beautiful place such a mess?

## A Year of Trash

In just 1 year, people all over the world throw away 2.48 million tons (2.25 million mt) of plastic bottles and jars. We use between 500 billion and 1 trillion plastic bags. In 2011, Asia alone produced about 196 million tons (177.8 million mt) of paper and cardboard products. A lot of it ends up as trash.

When people see trash somewhere, they're more likely to leave their own garbage, too. That's just one reason why it's important to always clean up after yourself!

The beach isn't just a vacation spot. It's a **habitat**. Your backyard is another habitat. Is there a colony of ants in the ground? How about a family of squirrels running around? There may be trees, bushes, and flowers in your backyard habitat.

Pollution is when harmful matter is put into the air, soil, or water. Trash, smoke, and chemical waste are all types of pollution.

In the many kinds of habitats all over the world, there's a lot of pollution. Let's take a look at how pollution is created and what kind of **havoc** it causes in some of these habitats.

## An Old, Old Problem

Pollution problems aren't new! Ancient Romans raised cows, goats, and sheep. These animals produced the gas methane, which is known today as a greenhouse gas. In China, rice fields also gave off methane. Wood smoke from fires polluted the air. In addition, people dumped garbage into rivers or left it piled on the ground. Sadly, these are all still sources of pollution.

When rain falls on garbage or polluted materials, it mixes with harmful matter and flows into nearby habitats.

# POISONING THE POLAR BEARS

Starting around 1929, chemicals called polychlorinated biphenyls (PCBs) were used to make motor oil, plastic, paint, and other products. Some PCBs leaked into the water—and over time have even moved to places like the Arctic. PCBs get into tiny animals, which are eaten by small fish. Larger fish eat the smaller fish, and so on up the food chain. Each animal takes in more of the harmful matter, so the animal at the top of the food chain takes in the most. In the Arctic, that's the polar bear.

Today, polar bears' food is making them sick and weak. Some can't survive. And it's all because of pollution.

## The Good News!

Some countries started banning PCBs around 1980. In 2004, the making of PCBs was banned around the world. Scientists in Norway have been studying some polar bears. From 1998 until 2008, the amount of PCBs in the bears fell over 50 percent. The bears are getting healthier. The ban is working!

Seals are a polar bear's main food. If a seal has been poisoned with PCBs, the polar bear will also be poisoned.

# REINDEER ALERT

In the northern **taiga** regions of Mongolia, reindeer herders are struggling to keep their animals safe and healthy. Mining and logging are destroying the reindeers' fields, and in some areas, the herders have lost their land because of the mines. These mines have dumped chemicals into the water, and it's no longer safe to drink.

The global climate change caused in part by pollution around the world is making summers in the area hotter, too. The reindeer don't do as well in the warmer temperatures. Reindeer are being bitten by more ticks and dying of diseases they catch from them.

## The Trouble with Tourists

Tourists like to see the reindeer and experience the herders' way of life. While this helps the herders' community earn money, tourists have added problems, too. Tourist camps are set up close to the reindeer fields. The herders change their animals' **migration** routes so the tourists can more easily see them—even if it means grazing in one place too long or missing out on the best pastures.

reindeer with herder

Global climate change is the gradual increase of Earth's average temperatures. A major cause of it is pollution. The taiga region the reindeer live in isn't the only habitat that's being harmed by the change.

# RAIN, RAIN, GO AWAY

Rain is good for flowers, animals, and people, right? Not always. When **fossil fuels** are burned, such as those used at a power plant, they give off toxic gases. These gases rise into the atmosphere, where they mix with water droplets in the air. When the water falls to Earth as rain, it's full of harmful matter. This is known as acid rain.

**1** **harmful gases rise into the atmosphere**

Acid rain damages the soil, so crops don't grow well. Animals and people face food shortages as acid rain pollutes water habitats. High amounts of acid rain can stop most fish eggs from hatching. Fish, frogs, shellfish, and even insects are harmed or killed by acid rain.

Acid rain is the result of air pollution—such as the harmful gases released by cars and planes—entering the water cycle.

2 **gases mix with water droplets and form clouds**

3 **acid rain falls**

4 **plants, animals, and soil are polluted by acid rain**

## Rain on the Roads

Acid rain hurts people's habitats, too! Acid rain damages our roadways, making them less safe. It falls on cars, leaving tiny marks. The rain eats away at buildings and statues. Acid rain weakens the metal bolts that hold bridges together. Some bridges have fallen down because of this!

# OH MY—OIL!

Oil spills destroy habitats. This dangerous pollution comes from tankers on the water, overland pipeline leaks, and oil-drilling platforms at sea.

When an animal's fur or feathers get coated with slick or sticky oil, the animal can't stay warm. They might not be able to float, fly, or walk. When animals try to lick off the oil, they swallow the toxins in it. Oil spills kill some animals, like fish, and then other animals have no food.

In 2000, an oil spill near Cape Town, South Africa, caused so much damage to the African penguins' habitat, the birds had to be airlifted off their island home! More than 10,000 adult African penguins were rescued.

## Gulf Coast Animals

A huge oil spill in the Gulf of Mexico in 2010 harmed or killed many animals. At least 6,000 birds, 600 sea turtles, and 150 sea mammals died. Workers cleaned up and released over 1,200 birds, 450 sea turtles, and 5 mammals, but the toxins from the oil will affect their habitats for years to come.

Oil spills cause long-lasting damage to habitats. Some habitats never recover.

rescued penguin is cleaned of oil

# UNHEALTHY HONEYBEES

Honeybees live in colonies all over the world. And they're having pollution problems everywhere! Scientists think fumes from car engines may be harming the bees' brains. They become confused and can't find their way back to their hive.

Flowers give off scents that draw bees. Scientists think air pollution may be stopping the scents from traveling, and the bees can't smell their sweetness. Then, the bees don't land on the flowers, don't drink the **nectar**, and don't take the **pollen** to other flowers. Without pollen, no new fruits or vegetables form. New plants don't grow, and the world has fewer crops. In addition, the bees die of hunger!

## Helpful Honeybees

Scientists in Frankfurt, Germany, set up honeybee colonies at the Frankfurt Airport to study pollution. They're examining the honey made by the bees to see if it has pollutants in it. They reported in July 2011 that the honey was safe to eat! But they aren't sure if that means there's little pollution at the airport or if the bees store the harmful matter in their bodies.

Scientists have found that observing plants and animals can tell a lot about the health of a habitat. Studies like the one in Germany are becoming more common.

honeybee drinking nectar

# MOUNTAINS OF TRASH

Adventurers love to climb Mount Everest. It's the tallest mountain in the world—and it's on the way to becoming the most polluted! Climbers leave used oxygen tanks and food wrappers behind as they climb. Some leave tents and clothes. It's so cold on the mountain that the debris doesn't break down.

Everest isn't the only messy mountain. Trash from hikers and campers is a problem all over the world. Wild animals may eat some of the trash, often causing them to get sick. The lure of food brings animals too close to people, and both could be hurt!

## The Breakdown

This chart shows how long it takes for trash to break down.

| trash | time to break down |
|---|---|
| fruit peels | 30 days |
| wool sock, scarf, glove | 1–5 years |
| rubber boot or shoe sole | 50–80 years |
| aluminum can | 80–200 years |
| plastic drink bottle | 450 years |
| glass bottle | up to 1 million years |

One climber said the top of Mount Everest was "disgustingly polluted, with garbage leaking out of glaciers."

# THE GREAT PACIFIC GARBAGE PATCH

The biggest garbage dump in the world is in the Pacific Ocean! Garbage from ships at sea is some of it, but most comes from land. Most of it is plastic.

To many sea creatures, the debris looks like food. When eaten, plastic remains in animals' stomachs without breaking down. There's no room for real food, so the animals starve to death. Scientists think more than 1 million sea animals die like this every year.

The Pacific Ocean debris floats, so it may carry sea creatures away from their natural habitats, too. This movement upsets the balance in both the animals' new habitat and the one they left behind.

## Garbage in the Deep Sea

Scientists have found trash in deep ocean canyons and on the seafloor. Most of the debris is plastic. Half of that plastic is plastic bags, which can choke sea animals. There are also cans, rope, glass, clothing, and shoes. Because of the lack of sunlight and warmth, the debris doesn't break down quickly. It will be there for many years.

tiny plastic pieces found in the Great Pacific Garbage Patch

The Great Pacific Garbage Patch is so large, it can be seen from space! Here's some of the garbage that's been found there.

# NOISY WATERS

About 15 years ago, the US Navy began testing a new kind of **sonar** to find enemy submarines. The sonar makes very loud noises in the water. Add in the noise from the engines of motorboats, Jet Skis, and cruise ships, and many **marine** habitats are facing terrible noise pollution problems.

Whales and dolphins use sound to find food, find their way, and "talk" to each other. The sonar and loud motors disrupt their communications. It confuses them, and they get lost. Many whales washed up on beaches when the navy was first testing the sonar. Scientists think the noises may also damage animals' ears.

## Sound Off

Scientists are studying how noise affects marine animals and trying to make quieter engines. Some places ban the use of engines near animal habitats. In 2008, a group filed a lawsuit about the navy's use of sonar near California, saying it was harming marine habitats. The Supreme Court ruled that the navy had to use certain precautions when training with the sonar.

sailors in a submarine using sonar

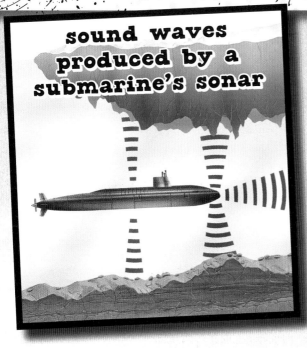

**sound waves produced by a submarine's sonar**

Sound travels for thousands of miles through the water, so this kind of pollution can certainly cause havoc!

# SPACE JUNK

There's even pollution in outer space! When spacecraft launch, parts break away, and some go into **orbit** above Earth. Broken **satellites** are also in orbit. Sometimes two spacecraft crash or a spacecraft explodes. Debris that's high above Earth may orbit for a century or more!

Orbiting space debris is a danger to spacecraft. Every piece of debris is traveling at a very high speed. Even a small piece of debris can cause damage if it hits a spacecraft—and the collision would cause even more debris!

Can space pollution hurt Earth? Most of it that's close enough to fall toward the planet burns up in the atmosphere. But sometimes debris falls to Earth's surface.

## Cleaning Up Space

Space agencies around the world are working together to find ways to make spacecraft that create less debris. Right now it's too expensive to remove space junk, but scientists are hoping to do it in the future. They also want to find ways to send satellites and rockets into orbit without creating more debris.

You can see space debris
with a telescope!

# REDUCIN' POLLUTION

You can help reduce pollution. If you're already doing some of these things—keep it up! If you're not, then start today!

- **Reduce:** Use less packaging. Turn off lights when you're not in the room. Walk or ride your bike instead of asking a parent to drive you.

- **Reuse:** Use china and silverware instead of plastic. Take cloth bags to the grocery store and for other errands. Use cardboard boxes over and over. Save rainwater in barrels and use it to water your plants.

- **Recycle:** Put plastic, paper, and cardboard in recycling bins. Donate old, but still usable, toys, clothes, and other things instead of putting them in the trash.

**recycling bins**

## Make Compost!

Leftover fruits and vegetables make great **compost**. So do coffee grounds, old flowers, grass clippings, and leaves. You put these materials in a pile on the ground or in a special bin. Add water. The materials will rot. Then you can use the compost on your garden.

compost bin

Try reducing pollution with your friends and family! Many areas have cleanup groups that are sponsored by local government, businesses, or other groups. Scout troops and churches often have neighborhood cleanup projects, too. Consider joining one—or start your own at your school or in your neighborhood.

Here are some things you could do:

- pick up trash at the park;
- hold a recycling fair at the school or library;
- rake leaves from streets, sidewalks, or storm drain grates;
- clean up the shore if you live near a body of water.

## Clean the Bay Day

Every year, thousands of volunteers clean up the Chesapeake Bay area on Clean the Bay Day. These volunteers pick up hundreds of thousands of pounds of trash. They work all along the 500 miles (805 km) of shoreline of the Virginia and Maryland coasts. This event has been going on for 25 years!

Every piece of trash you pick up from the beach, trail, or street helps Earth stay cleaner and reduces habitat havoc.

**compost:** matter made from rotten food and cut grass. It's added to soil to make it better.

**debris:** the remains of something

**fossil fuel:** matter formed over millions of years from plant and animal remains that is burned for power

**habitat:** the natural place where an animal or plant lives

**havoc:** great destruction or confusion

**marine:** having to do with the ocean

**migration:** moving from place to place at certain times of year

**nectar:** a sweet liquid made by flowering plants

**orbit:** to travel in a circle or oval around something, or the path used to make that trip

**pollen:** a fine yellow dust produced by plants

**satellite:** an object that circles Earth in order to collect and send information or aid in communication

**sonar:** a machine that uses sound waves to find things in a body of water

**taiga:** the cold, forested area that begins where the tundra ends

# For More Information

## Books

Knight, Geof. *Plastic Pollution.* Chicago, IL: Heinemann Library, 2012.

McKenzie, Precious. *Cleaning Up the Earth.* Vero Beach, FL: Rourke Publishing, 2012.

Mileham, Rebecca. *Global Pollution.* Mankato, MN: NewForest Press, 2011.

## Websites

### Habitat Conservation
*www.nmfs.noaa.gov/habitat/*
Read about the National Oceanic and Atmospheric Association's efforts to save marine and other habitats.

### Habitat Destruction
*www.worldanimalfoundation.net/f/HabitatDestruction.pdf*
Find out more about how human activities can cause havoc in natural habitats.

### Habitat Loss
*www.nwf.org/Wildlife/Threats-to-Wildlife/Habitat-Loss.aspx*
Learn more about the causes of habitat pollution and how we can help solve the problems that pollution causes.

# Index